Billy Ivey

Visit Small Stories online at smallstoriesstudio.com.

Napkinisms

For information about special discounts for bulk purchases, please contact Small Stories Studio at info@smallstoriesstudio.com, or call 205-757-7825.

Library of Congress Cataloging-in-Publication Data
ISBN 979-8-218-33196-2
Printed in the United States of America.

Sometimes, our biggest mistakes can turn out to be our greatest blessings.

I should know. I have five kids.

This book is dedicated to at least three of them.

Off we go...

A few years ago, I started writing notes to my kids.
Lunch notes.
On napkins.
OK, they were actually paper towels.
Toe-may-toe, Toe-mah-toe.
Papertowelisms sounded dumb, so here we are.

I'm not the first person to do this. Chances are you have given and/
or, but probably *and* received a lunch note at some point in your life.

It's what we do.

So, anyway, my wife – as wonderful and beautiful and perfect in
almost every way as she is – is not a morning person. Not even a
little bit. Because of that, I usually get the kids up and off to school,
and part of that process is packing lunches.

So, for a bunch of years now, I have been including a note alongside
peanut butter and jelly sandwiches, bruised bananas, Doritos, Oreos,
and fruit snacks if they're lucky. They love it when I do this. I found
out recently that my now eighteen-year-old daughter has been
collecting the notes I write for her for years.

She probably has 400 of them in a hatbox under her bed.

One morning, I wrote a note that I thought was particularly

insightful, so I took a picture of it and posted it to Instagram and Facebook, and, *voila*! "Napkinisms" was born.

The response on-line, was surprising — baffling, really — but delightful, so I started posting the kids' notes every day.

Over and over and over. Day after day after day... I was writing notes to my heathens and posting the notes for the whole world to see... Or at least the few hundred Instagram followers I had gained.

Turns out, these notes that I intended for my children were impacting other people, too. Over and over and over again. My mind was blown. I had friends and family in other parts of the country sending me messages that they'd seen these silly (paper towels) shared by friends of friends of friends in Kansas, California, Little Rock, Michigan, and towns in Texas and Iowa I'd never even heard of.

Soon, my followers online went from a few hundred to several *thousand*!

These notes – these ridiculous "Napkinisms" being scribbled on Bounty Select-A-Size Paper Towels were kind of going viral! These bad dad-joke notes on which the key messages often include topics such as diarrhea, vomit, poop, boogers, toenail clippings, and subtle jabs at my wife's cooking were... out there for the world to see.

Today, hundreds of thousands of people from all over the world have seen these stupid things. But it turns out they might not be all that stupid after all.

Mindblowingly simple and sophomoric as they are, my Napkinisms have connected with and touched people in seemingly hundreds of thousands of ways — some people laugh; some cry; and one lady even wrote and told me that she was reconsidering her decision NOT to have kids, because she, too, wanted to "write notes like these one day."

What. In. The. World?

Please know in your hearts that I do not think decisions to either have or not have kids — *to bring human beings into the world* — should teeter on having the opportunity to write messages on paper towels, but that was a pretty powerful message to receive.

And more and more powerful stories and testimonies and comments and real-life examples of perspective-changing and day-making moments are being shared day after day.

But, all I'm doing is writing bad dad jokes and silly messages to my kids, right?

Maybe.

My wife once said, "Sweetheart," she calls me sweetheart when she's about to say something I probably won't like. She said, "Sweetheart, I don't think it's *what* you are writing. It's *that* you're writing."

And you know what? She was right.

The power of Napkinisms is not in *what* I write on the Select-A-Size Bounty Paper Towels (product placement) with fine-tip Sharpie (product placement) markers, it's *that* I write them at all.

Somehow these things are finding the places they need to be, and days are changed because of them. I don't know how it works, but it does. My friend, Brad Montague, once said that "even a small message, crafted in love, will find where it needs to be," and I couldn't agree more.

The greatest lesson I have learned throughout all of this is the fact that *you don't have to do something grand to do something great.*

Read that again: *You don't have to do something grand to do something great*

That's true in your home; it's true in your business; it's true with your families and friends; it's just plain true in life.

Take it from me… The napkin guy… the, um, the guy who writes stuff on paper towels.

You're gonna change the world…

These are Napkinisms.

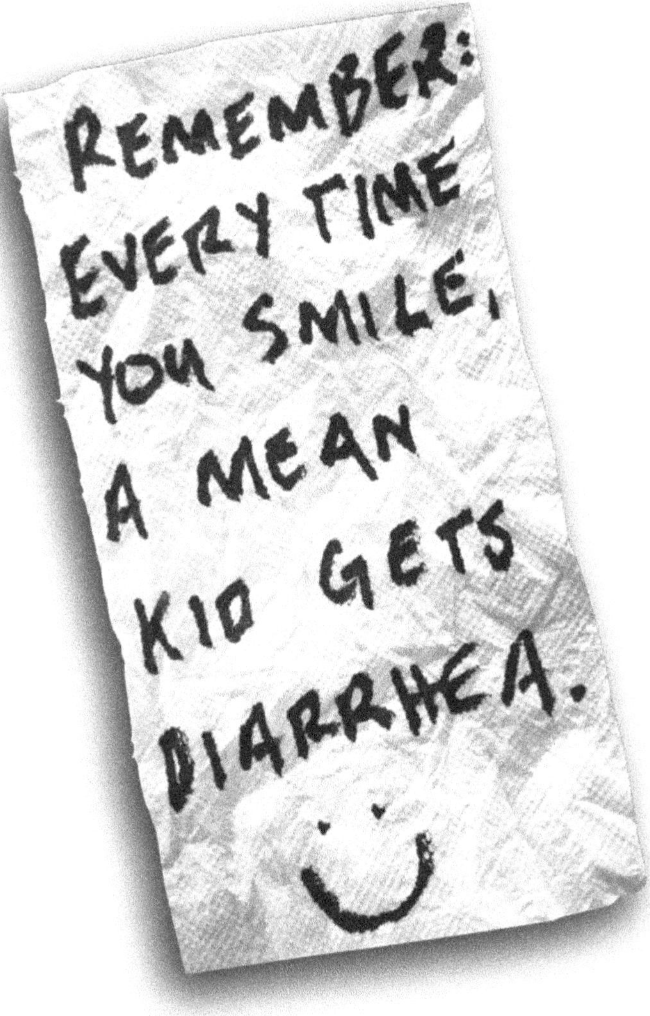
REMEMBER:
EVERY TIME
YOU SMILE,
A MEAN
KID GETS
DIARRHEA.

One of my sons was being bullied at school. Not the physical kind of bullying… The worse kind. The kind that hurts a lot more and stays with you a lot longer than scraped knuckles and blackened eyes. He was being picked on and made fun of and told over and over again that he wasn't good enough or cool enough or… enough-enough. We sure showed them.

Seriously. If you had to pick between making an "A" on a Math test, or eating a doughnut, which would you choose?

Perspective, y'all. Find what's good.

YOU MIGHT
NOT BE AS
SMART AS
YOUR SISTER,
BUT SHE
CAN'T EAT
GLUTEN, SO...
YOU WIN!

PLEASE EAT
ALL OF YOUR
CARROTS.
THEY ARE
SUPPOSED TO
MAKE YOU SMART
AND YOU NEED
ALL THE HELP
YOU CAN GET.

Nutrition is more importanter than most people realize.

Raise your hand if you've purchased more than 300 phone chargers, but can never find one when you need it. I've threatened violence on my children. I've threatened military school. I've threatened inviting all of their friends to follow me on TikTok. But they still take my chargers.

At least they used to. I've started wearing tighty-whities.

STOP TAKING MY PHONE CHARGER, AND I'LL STOP TAKING YOU TO SCHOOL IN MY UNDERWEAR.

I'M SORRY I
YELLED AT YOU
THIS MORNING.
I WAS JUST
PRACTICING FOR
LATER WHEN WE
DO HOMEWORK.

I love my people. I really do.
But doing homework with my people makes me
not like my people very much.
Or Math teachers.

They pee on the *walls*, y'all.

FYI: THE HANDS THAT HAD TO CLEAN UP AFTER YOU THIS MORNING ARE THE SAME HANDS THAT MADE THIS LUNCH. THINK ABOUT THAT THE NEXT TIME YOU PEE ALL OVER THE BATHROOM.

THE BLACK SPOTS
ON YOUR BANANA
ARE KIND OF LIKE
BATTLE SCARS.
YOU ARE ABOUT TO
EAT A VERY, VERY
BRAVE BANANA.

At our house, a bushel — and yes, I mean a bushel — of bananas can be eaten in roughly 37 minutes. Or, they turn into sacks of porridge-looking goo that don't get thrown away until someone asks the very specific question: "why are these little flies all over the place?" Or, "Does something smell musty to y'all? What is that?"

13 dollars?

My Mom used to visit every so often. She'd come in for the kids' ballgames, recitals, and other events where her presence was often undervalued, and always marginally appreciated by those she came to honor. "I'm so proud of you! Great job! You are so talented! Mimi loves you so much…" She'd pour out her accolades and delight with the excitement of a raving fan, sometimes even following up the charge with, "can I have your autograph?"

She always came bearing gifts, too. But not like *"real"* gifts. She'd bring plastic things. Gadgets, knick-knacks, trinkets, baubles, and tchotchke she'd pick up at the Kangaroo gas station or Dollar Tree between here and her home in Newnan, Georgia. Oh, and candy. Good lord. Always with the candy. She'd spend a month's social security on Gummy Worms.

"Tell you what," I'd say. "Next time, just bring us $300 for the cavities we're gonna have to get filled, OK?"

And I was only half-joking. Her incessant "gift" giving was a little bit annoying. "Why do you bring them these silly things? You *do* know this stuff breaks before you even make it back to your house, don't you? It's kind of a waste of money."

She'd purse her lips and smile. "Oh, let them enjoy it," she'd say. "Even if it's just for a few minutes. Haven't you ever heard 'it's the thought that counts'?"

Yes. Yes I have. I'd mumble to myself. *So, how about thinking of something else next time…*

No matter how hard we'd try to convince her that she was wasting her money; buying things the kids would never use again; and really kind of pissing us off by going against our wishes and continuing to fill our trash bins with useless crap… she'd always show up with a sackful of Gummy Bears, cap guns, action figures, hair bows, and .99-cent knock-off Barbie dolls.

And she was always trying to give me money! Always. Big bills. Small bills. Change from the bottom of her purse…

"Mom, for cripe's sake, I don't need the money. Stop. I don't need it. You feel bad? Why do you feel bad? Trouble? You're no trouble. Why do you think you're trouble? You're family. Stop apologizing for coming to visit. No. I'm not taking your money. And don't give it to the kids. They don't need it either. They don't need anything. We're covered up as it is already. My gosh, there's enough candy in there to kill an Oompa-Loompa. I'm not going to tell you again. No. I'm not mad. Why do you think I'm mad? I'm just saying. We don't need your money. YOU need your money. Keep it. Put it back in your purse and we'll see you in a few weeks. Go. We'll see you later. Leave. See you soon. I love you, too. We all do. Bye. Thank you. See you later. Buh-bye…"

One time, a few years ago, my daughter and I went out to the car after one of Mom's visits, and I found a wadded-up paper towel in the driver's seat. I opened it up and found several bills crumpled inside and a note that simply read: *Love you.*

After shaking my head and rolling my eyes, I put the paper towel in the cup holder and started to back out of the driveway. "How much money is that?" My daughter asked, picking up the folded bills and counting. "It's thirteen dollars," she said. "Why would Mimi give you thirteen dollars?"

Exactly, I thought to myself. *How weird is that? Why in the world would she give me thirteen do…?* And then it hit me, sure as I am typing the words today. She gave me thirteen dollars because that's all she had.

She gave me everything.

If she'd been able to find an ink pen, peppermint, Band-Aid, paperclip, coupon, or gift card in her pocketbook, she would've wrapped that up in a paper towel, too.

She gave me everything.
She gave *us* everything.

What a woman.
Gosh, we miss you, Mom.

#lovelikemimi

NO ONE LOVES
YOU MORE THAN I
DO. EXCEPT FOR
JESUS. AND MOM.
AND PROBABLY MIMI.
OH! AND THAT WEIRD
LADY FROM CHURCH
WHO KISSES YOU
ON THE MOUTH...

I LOVE YOU.
EVEN THOUGH
YOU STILL
SAY "LIBERRY."

:(

She's in college now.
The other day, she went to the business liberry.

The sun came up again today. *How cool is that?*

WE ASK
FOR MIRACLES
EVERY DAY,
BUT FORGET
THAT EVERY
DAY IS
A MIRACLE.

ALWAYS FINISH
WHAT YOU START.
THIS IS ONE
OF THE MOST
IMPORTANT THINGS
YOU WILL EVER

I like this one. It reminds me of a

They teach it different these days. And I don't get it.
And neither do my kids from the looks of things.
So, it's *always* the rainy season at my house.

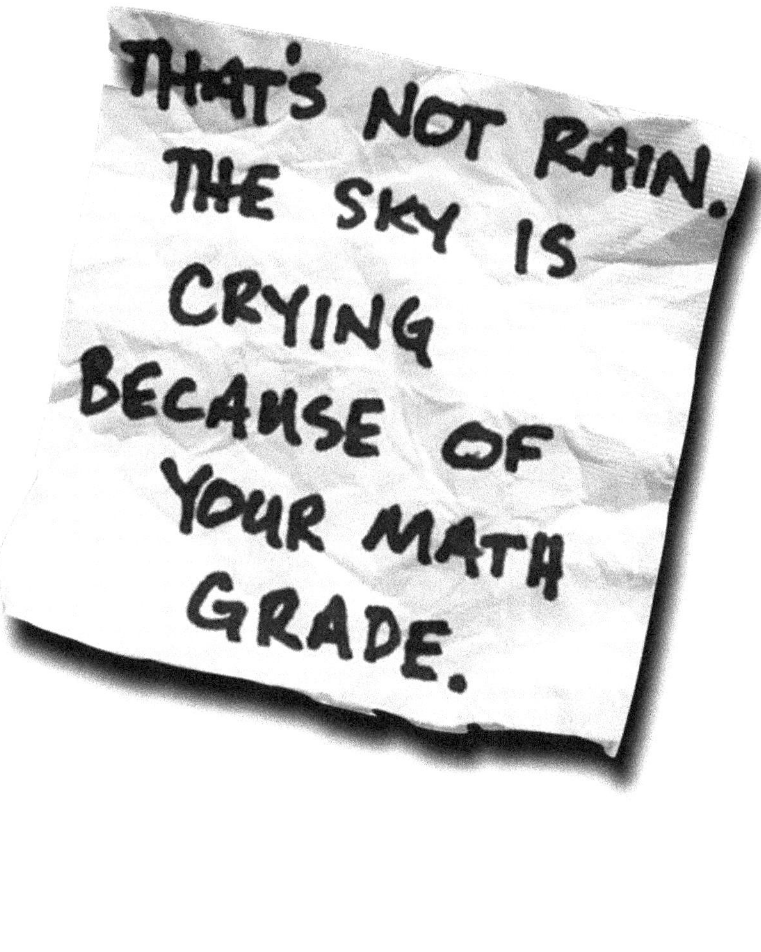
THAT'S NOT RAIN.
THE SKY IS
CRYING
BECAUSE OF
YOUR MATH
GRADE.

STOP
COMPLAINING
ABOUT THINGS
THAT MOST
PEOPLE WILL
NEVER BE
BLESSED TO
KNOW THEY
DON'T LIKE.

Broccoli, for example.

Now, I realize this is just a new and current and possibly more patronizing way to say the whole "starting kids in Africa" thing, but that obviously didn't work. They *still* don't eat broccoli and there are *still* starving kids in Africa… and this particular note has more to do with the fact that we got the boys an Xbox instead of a PS5, and that was three years ago, and they still complain about it to this day, even though they all have jobs and could definitely buy themselves the PS5, and that settles it… we're eating broccoli for dinner.

National Daughter's Day is in October every year, and I think that's about the dumbest thing I've ever heard. At least on National Pizza Day, National Ice Cream Day, National Beer Day, and National Seafood Bisque Day (which also, and super coincidentally, occurs in October) you get to eat and drink stuff and not feel bad about it.

These girls are gonna kill me, you guys.

YOU
CAN'T
SPELL

DAUGHTERS

WITHOUT

"UGH."

DO NOT
EVER TRUST
A TOOT THE
DAY AFTER
TACO NIGHT.
I'M NOT
KIDDING.
:|

This is the most important napkin note I or anyone else has ever written. It just is. Especially on Wednesdays.

I once gave a speech to a roomful of accountants. Jealous? Anyway, it went about as well as you might expect a guy talking about napkins to a group of accountants might go. But there was one guy in the front row who was particularly miserable.

For a solid hour, he stared at me like he wanted to hurt me, and I developed a great hatred of this guy in my heart. After the event, he came up to me and handed me a note…

Doctors found a
volleyball size tumor
on my mom Friday.
90% chance its very
aggressive cancer.

~~Bs~~ Her oncology appointment
is ~~tomorros~~ tomorrow.

I sent her your facebook
page.

It made her laugh.

Her name is Kathy

God bless

Foof.

I don't know this guy's name, but his Mom's name is Kathy. And it turns out Kathy and her son were having a pretty rough day.

IF WE COULD
SEE THE
WHOLE STORY
AND NOT JUST
THE CHAPTER
WE ARE IN,
I BET WE
WOULD ALL BE
NICER TO
EACH OTHER.

IT'S
NATIONAL
BOSS DAY.
Y'ALL BE
NICE TO
MOM. :)

Sometimes, I say, "yes, ma'am," and I'm not even joking.

This, too, shall pass.

SOME DAYS
ARE LIKE
POOPING.
JUST PUSH
THROUGH,
AND YOU'LL
FEEL BETTER
WHEN
IT'S OVER.

BE A
LIGHT,
KID.

My favorite Bible verse is Matthew 5:16 — "Let your light so shine among men that they might see your good works and glorify your Father in heaven."

I love this so much because it is both specific and super-vague: *Let your light shine. Got it. OK, but how? Where? When?*

Ahhh, that's the cool part. You don't have to be a doctor, lawyer, teacher, preacher, writer, accountant, plumber, or… whatever… to make a difference.

You just gotta be a light, and the whole world will see.

This was almost the worst break-up ever.

I CAN'T
LOVE YOU
~~ANYMORE.~~
ANY MORE.

:)

TELLING
PEOPLE THAT
THEY ARE
LOVED IS
POWERFUL.
SHOWING
THEM WILL
CHANGE THE
WORLD.

A friend of mine sent me a note once in response to these ridiculous notes, and it kind of changed the way I think about everything.

He wrote: *These notes on napkins are not just words on napkins, and I hope you understand that. If nothing else, these things are an outward expression of what you tell your kids every night before they go to bed or you hang up the phone. These notes are powerful. Keep writing them. Keep showing them. It's going to change their lives and they are going to change the world someday.*

I tell my family that I love them every day.
I wish I showed them more.

Being a dad is great, I think.

Being a dad is great. It's fun! You know what else is fun, probably? *Not* being a dad. I can't be one-hundred-percent sure of the latter, because I don't remember a single second before these people came kicking and screaming into my life. But I bet you could line up a thousand not-dads and ask them if they have fun, and just about every one of them would cut their eyes to the left real quick as if looking for the punchline, and then huff: *Um, duh-uh.*

But, whatever. Good for them. All I know is that I am super-happy being a dad. Of course, I never intended to have *five* kids. I wanted two. Still do sometimes. But the good Lord thought it'd be neat to throw three more in there, so what are you gonna do?

Being a dad is great. Seriously. I mean it.

Sure, it's exhausting. And expensive. And terrifying. And debilitating. And expensive. And frustrating. And maddening, which is not the same thing as frustrating, but almost — there's just a little more crazy thrown in — and very expensive. And gut-wrenching. And sad at times. And anxiety-ridden. And sleepless. And ulcer-inducing. And expensive. And, sure, it costs a lot of money. But I wouldn't have it any other way.

These five, incredible creatures bless my life in ways that not-dads can't possibly imagine. You know, what with the 73 activities they are involved in every week. And the homework. All that freaking homework. And the doctor and dentist and orthodontist appointments. And the eating of all of the food that their mom *just* bought, like 13 minutes ago, even though they were told that we have to cut back on eating so much food because we can't go back to the grocery store until after payday because the next several weeks are going to be pretty tight financially. And the missing of the school bus because they can't find their shoes and so now I'm late for yet another meeting, and the "I have five kids" excuse is getting really old. And the pubescent hormones. And the holy crap, tuition is due again? And the wet towels left on the floor. Again. And the piles and piles and unrelenting piles of laundry. And the...

He looks kind of like me, doesn't he? Her smile is just like her mama's. It really does light up the room. He's so smart. Good grief, I love to watch her dance. He made the baseball team! She's doing really well in school. He's a reader, that one. She cleaned out the dishwasher without even being asked. When he gets tired, he twirls his hair. I love how she loves Jesus. His freckles come out in the summer. She applied to that job all on her own. He asks the most fascinating questions. He's hilarious. She's goofy as all get-out. He has such a sweet spirit. She's a fiery one. She's turning into a real beauty. He's kind. She's compassionate. He's so loving. He wants the best for everyone. She really gets it. They love each other. They're for each other...

And I've never loved anyone or anything any more than this...

Best. Job. Ever.

I LOVE BEING
YOUR DAD. IT'S
KIND OF LIKE
BEING YOUR MOM
EXCEPT SHE DOES
EVERYTHING AND
I STILL GET SOME
CREDIT FOR YOU
BEING AWESOME.
BEST. JOB. EVER.

CHILDREN
WHO CHEW
WITH THEIR
MOUTHS OPEN
GROW UP
TO BE
LONELY.
I'M JUST
SAYIN'.
:.

For the most part, my kids are well-behaved, considerate, and thoughtful when it comes to making others feel seen, heard, and appreciated. But something happens to them when we sit down at the dinner table. Something sinister and "unholy."

They look and sound like cows gnawing their cud every evening as we break bread together.

God almighty and I are working on the disdain I have for my offspring when they eat… but I'm afraid we've got a long way to go.

I gave her the answers and she *still* screwed up the ACT.

BACADCBB
ACDBBACD
DCCAABD
BABACCDA
DDABBCCA
BACBDCAB
DDCAABAC
CCBADDB
BAACBAD
ABBCBDA

LOVE IS
A VERB.
CONJUGATE
THE HECK
OUT OF IT
TODAY.

:)

Present Simple:
He, She, It: loves.

Present Continuous (Progressive):
I: am loving you. We, They: are loving. He, She, It: is loving.

Present Perfect:
I, You, We, They: have loved. He, She, It: has loved.

Past Simple:
I, You, We, They, He, She, It: loved.

Past Continuous:
I, He, She, It: was loving. He, She, We, They: were loving.

Past Perfect:
I, You, We, They, He, She, It: had loved.

And so on and so on, etc.

My wife and I have a friend who compliments people on things *most* people don't see… or at least they don't say out loud. "Oh, wow!" She might exclaim, walking past a stranger, "you have great shoulders…" Our friend is weird.

But is she, though? She'd never say to someone, "You're so pretty," because she sees more than that. She'd compliment the whole face. And that's awesome.

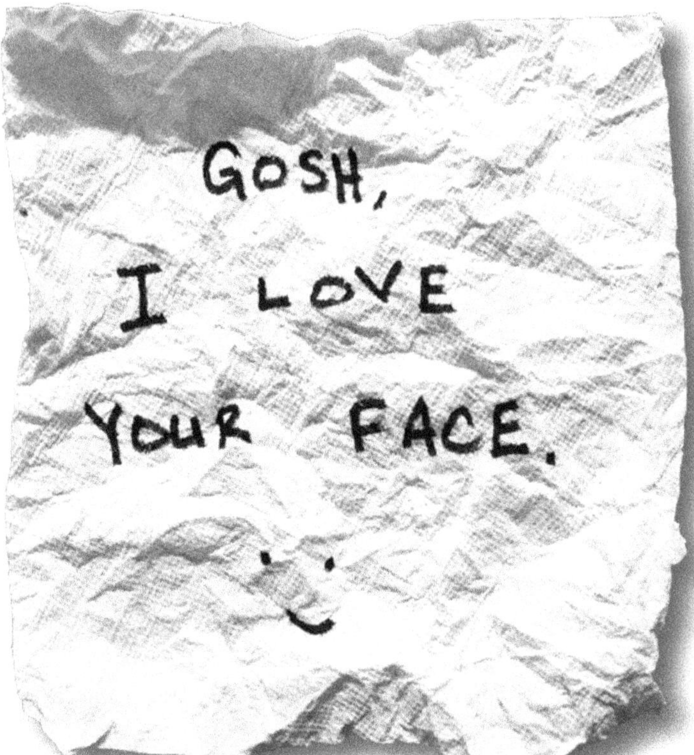
GOSH,
I LOVE
YOUR FACE.

THIS IS THE DAY
THE LORD HATH
MADE. LET US
REJOICE AND BE
GLAD NOBODY
REALLY SAYS
"HATH" ANY MORE.

I guess people with severe lisps might say 'hath,' but not on purpoth.

I used to think "kill 'em with kindness" was ridiculous… until I saw it in action. I mean, nobody *actually* died, but you should have seen the look on that inconsiderate jerk's face when I smiled and told him to have a great day. He almost choked on his fat tongue. I'm still working on this one, BTW.

BE
KIND
TO
MEAN
PEOPLE.
THEY
HATE
THAT
CRAP.

SMILE.
WORK HARD.
PRAY.
BELIEVE.
SERVE OTHERS.
STUDY.
DO GOOD.

DON'T EAT BOOGERS.

There are a lot of things kids need to learn and put into practice. These are paramount in my opinion.

Perpetually kind people have 23% less cortisol (the stress hormone… not to be confused with cortisone, which is the stuff you rub on minor skin irritations to get rid of the itchies) and age slower than the average population.

So, in summary, be nice and you might just get rid of that pesky rash, too! Wait…

MAKE EVERY DAY BETTER FOR SOMEONE OTHER THAN YOURSELF, AND YOURSELF WILL BECOME A BETTER SOMEONE EVERY DAY.

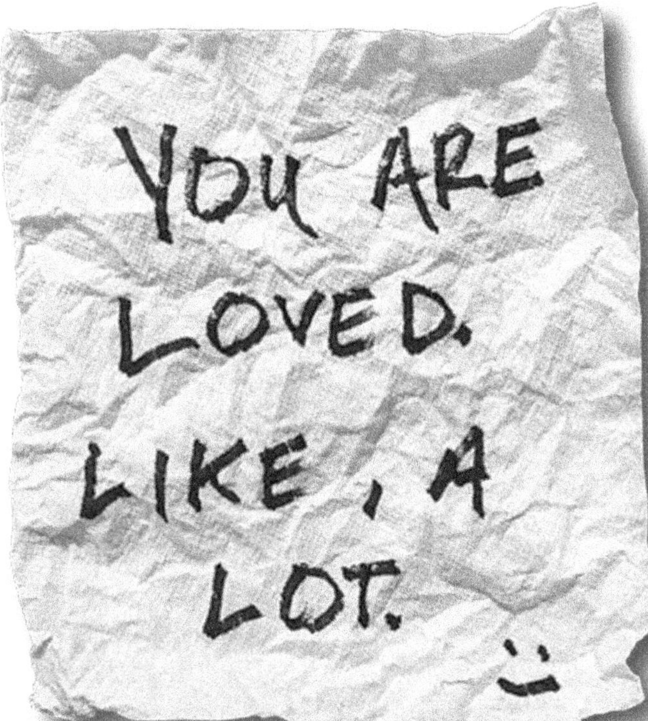
YOU ARE
LOVED.
LIKE, A
LOT.

Like, a lot-a lot. You. Are. Loved.

It's one of the easiest things to forget, but one of the most important things to remember. Even on your worst day. Even when things aren't going your way. Even when you don't even like yourself very much. Even when the world seems to be lining up to keep you down… and maybe even especially then… You are loved.

Birthdays, Christmas, Valentine's Day, National Women's Day, and pretty much when we need for her to go to the grocery store. Those are *all* her days, and that's kind of a lot of days if you think about it.

TODAY IS
NATIONAL
WOMEN'S DAY.
PLEASE TRY
TO REMEMBER
THAT YOUR
MOM IS ONE
OF THOSE
AND BE NICE
TO HER. :)

SORRY THIS
LUNCH IS
KIND OF LAME,
YOUR SISTER'S
SORORITY DUES
ARE COMING
UP AND WE
HAD TO
PRIORITIZE.

After posting this note — which is very, very real life, but also not — several folks responded negatively.

One lady commented: "Are you saying you are more interested in buying friends for your daughter than providing for your family?" I wanted to write back: "It's not that I am more interested in buying my daughter's friends than providing for my family, it's just a lot more expensive, so we we've just decided that the other kids can not eat on Tuesdays. It's fine. It's gonna be fine."

I do not love like.

PLEASE
LIKE, STOP,
LIKE, SAYING
LIKE, LIKE
AFTER EVERY,
LIKE, YOU
KNOW, LIKE
EVERY OTHER
WORD. :-(

MISERY
MIGHT LOVE
COMPANY,
BUT SO DOES
JOY. AND
JOY THROWS
MUCH BETTER
PARTIES. :)

A friend of mine — actually, we've never met in real life, but she's awesome and her art and poetry make me smile (also, we've exchanged DMs a few times, so *obvi* she's my friend) — named Lori Hetteen once wrote: *"I do not have ducks. Or a row. I have squirrels. And they are at a rave."* And for some reason I think about that every time I remember this note.

I think I'd like to go to a rave with some squirrels, wouldn't you?

I once had to read an article by some leadership guru guy who said that changing the phrase "have to" into "get to" made the biggest difference in his attitude every day and his productivity went up, like, 300%. I bet that's not true.

MAKE
TODAY A
GET TO
NOT A
HAVE TO
KIND OF
DAY.

:)

I WAS ABOUT
TO WRITE: I
LOVE YOU MORE
THAN YOUR
SISTER LOVES
TAYLOR SWIFT,
BUT IM PRETTY
SURE THAT'S
NOT TRUE.

SORRY. :-(

A female's love for TayTay is not limited to 17-year-old girls. My wife spent roughly a mortgage payment and what it costs to own one of the 46 surviving Imperial Fabergé Eggs on two tickets to the *Eras Tour*. And she'd do it again — every day and twice on Sundays.

I do not love *anything* that much.
Except her, maybe.

Maybe.

Jesus was perfect in personality, demeanor, character, conduct, and discipline. We can't really be all those things, but even trying for a day or two would be pretty awesome.

Maybe miracles *can* happen.

BE LIKE JESUS:
HANG OUT
WITH OUTCASTS.
TELL THE TRUTH.
LOVE EVERYONE.
LIVE FOR OTHERS.
AND ALWAYS
DO WHAT YOUR
DAD SAYS.

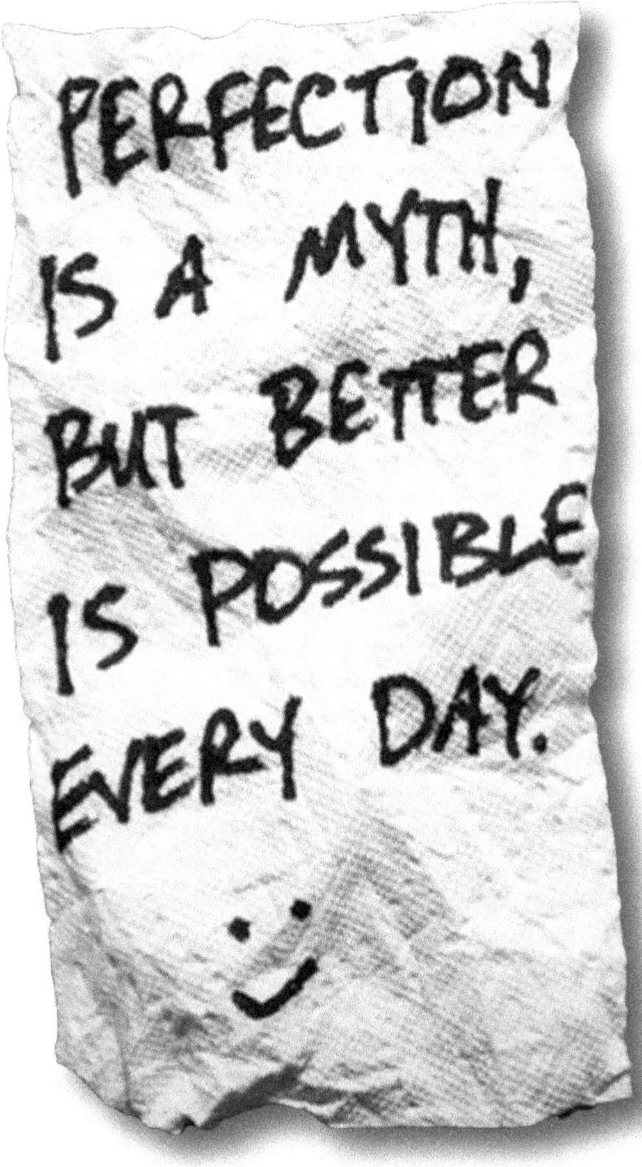
PERFECTION IS A MYTH, BUT BETTER IS POSSIBLE EVERY DAY.

This is like a quote you might see in a locker room or a pilates class being taught by a lady wearing spandex pants who probably shouldn't be wearing spandex pants, but good for her... she's confident in who she is. And who am I to judge someone who's *actually* exercising? Also, I had to look up what "pilates" is. It seems hard. Maybe I'll give it a try tomorrow?

Nah.

I once heard someone say that there is a fine line between loving others and condoning their behavior. I wholeheartedly *disagree*. That line could not be any *thicker* in my opinion. I don't have to love *what* you do; *what* you believe; or *how* you choose to live… to love you.

I love you *because* you are a broken, fallen, misguided, selfish, sinful, ne'er-do-well. Just. Like. Me.

LOVE
THY
NEIGHBOR.
EVERY.
SINGLE.
ONE.

BREAKING
NEWS:
YOUR BROTHER
FORGOT TO
SLAP THE
DOORFRAME
WHEN HE
LEFT THE
ROOM.

I haven't had a short kid becoming a tall(er) kid in several years, but, dude. There are, like, handprints on, like, every doorway in the whole house, bro.

You ever think about stuff like this? Surely he didn't nail bacon on his fist try! You're telling me this dude won the meat candy lottery without frying up a few roadkill entrails, or whatever, first?

The peanut butter and jelly guy is a close second place to the bacon guy, IMO. For the record, the peanut butter guy was *not* George Washington Carver as is often wrongly-claimed by people who obviously don't love peanut butter as much as me and mine. The inventor of peanut paste was actually a Canadian dude named Marcellus Gilmore Edson.*

Anyway, the bacon guy was probably a caveman or something, and God bless his nasty soul.

*I helped my now 20-year-old write a paper in 2016, but even if I hadn't had to do the research, I'd probably still know this fact, because… duh, peanut butter.

I BET THE
GUY WHO
DISCOVERED
BACON
TRIED SOME
PRETTY
GROSS STUFF
FIRST.

Don't just accept people in spite of differences. Love people because they are different.

I've learned more from people I disagree with than from folks who think about things the same way I do. How boring would life be without people who are wrong?

To all of the adults out there *not* living your dreams…
Congratulations. You grew up. Now, in no way am I saying that
dreams can't come true — ballerinas and pro baseball players exist
— but, at some point you accepted the fact that you'll never play
shortstop for the Atlanta Braves, and you became an accountant or
whatever. Good for you.

PART OF MY
ROLE AS A FATHER
IS TO TEACH YOU
ABOUT WHAT TO
EXPECT LATER IN
LIFE. THIS LUNCH
REPRESENTS
DISAPPOINTMENT.

WHEN YOU
LOOK FOR
THE GOOD
IN OTHERS,
IT'S EASIER
FOR OTHERS
TO FIND
THE GOOD
IN YOU. :)

One of my favorite people in the world is a guy named Gary Brandon. Gary has taught me more about creativity and marketing and branding and strategy than anyone else throughout my career. But there's something even more important that Gary has unknowingly taught me over the years.

He has always signed his emails, letters, text messages, or whatever with three, simple words, and if we'd *all* take his advice, I bet we'd all be a lot better off. Thanks, Gary.

"See the good."

Unless you can find one of those robots that has feelings and compassion and empathy and understands the complex needs of others, you should probably allow yourself to be a bit more vulnerable and love your neighbor as yourself. If you *can* find one of those robots, disregard the sentiments above, because that's about the coolest thing I've ever heard.

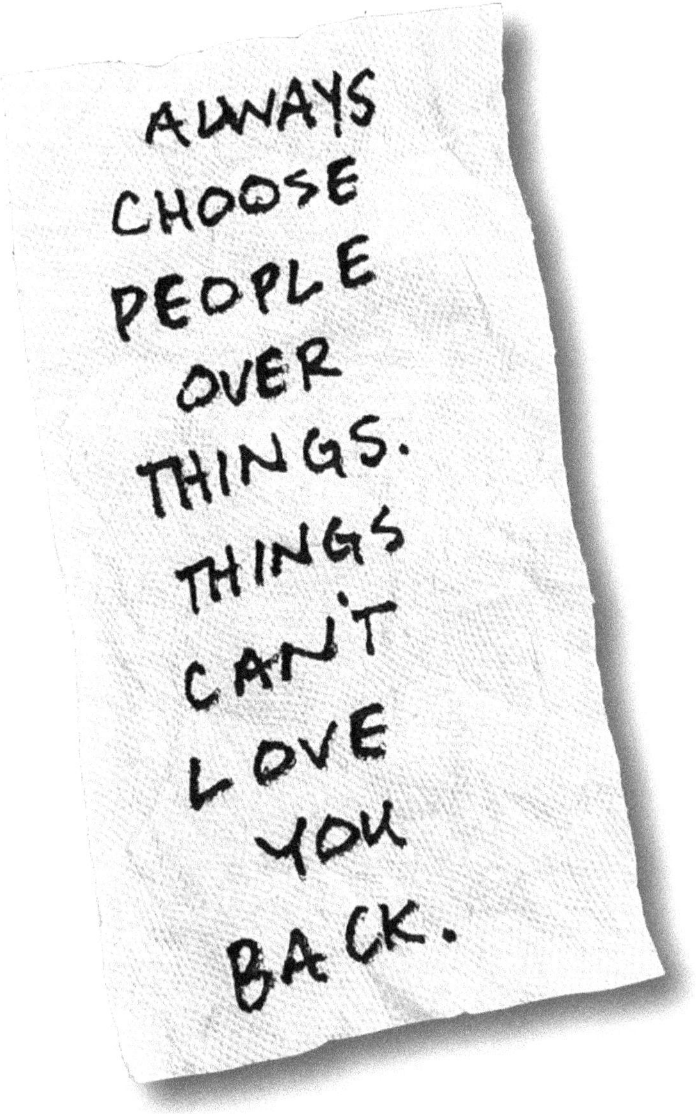
ALWAYS
CHOOSE
PEOPLE
OVER
THINGS.
THINGS
CAN'T
LOVE
YOU
BACK.

SOMETIMES OUR BIGGEST MISTAKES CAN TURN OUT TO BE OUR GREATEST BLESSINGS.

YOUR SISTER, FOR EXAMPLE.

‥ ‿

This is only *seems* mean. If you really think about it, this is one of the most endearing messages a kid could ever get. And if you don't agree, you obviously made better decisions as a 20-something year old than I did. Or, you know, you're probably a much better person than I am. That's neither here nor there. I love all of my mistakes very, very much. I *can* be very sweet.

One of the most difficult lessons to learn — and certainly to teach — is that dreaming big dreams is the only way to make big dreams come true. Mostly because that's false. Kind of like saying, "find something you love to do and you'll never work another day in your life." Never has something been more *untrue*. Dreams take hard work. Dreams only come to life when you wake up and do stuff! At least that's what I yell at 'em on their way out the door every morning. I also yell stupid stuff like what's on the next page…

DREAM
BIG DREAMS,
BUT KEEP
DOING THE
SMALL THINGS
THAT WILL
MAKE THEM
COME TRUE.

SWEET
CHI-1-1-1-
1-1-1-1-1-
1-1-1-1-1-
ILD OF
MYEEYINE.

As he was running to catch the school bus, I called out after him: "Your note today is brought to you by Axl Rose!" He stopped his trot, turned to me, and tilted his head like a dog trying its best to understand the command.

"What kind of rose?" He called back.

That afternoon, his homework was to listen to "Appetite for Destruction" on repeat until he got the joke and knew every word to "It's So Easy' and "Mr. Brownstone." And that, my friends, is called good parenting.

About 30 years ago, I was an English major.
I'm pretty sure this is called satire.

WHY I LOVE YOU
REASON #6,342:
YOU LOOK A
LOT LIKE ME,
AND I AM VERY
HANDSOME.

IT'S NEVER
TOO LATE
TO START
SOMETHING
NEW. UNLESS,
OF COURSE,
YOU WANTED
TO START
YESTERDAY.

Don't ever regret the things you didn't do yesterday. Today is *always* the best time to start something… mostly because there's another one tomorrow, so that means you can pretty much do whatever you want. Boom.

This child — this incredibly bright and creative and thoughtful child — says "amazeballs" when she thinks something is cool or great or awesome. Maybe even amazing. And I don't understand it.

The other day she exclaimed, "Oh, that's awesomesauce!" And my head popped completely off of my shoulders.

IT MAKES
MY SOUL
HURT WHEN
YOU SAY
THINGS LIKE
AMAZEBALLS.

HOPE
IS
REAL.
BUT
YOU
STILL
HAVE
TO
TRY.

I believe that God gave us *all* hearts and minds and courage and ideas and creativity and relationships and… all the tools necessary to bring about *everything* we hope for…

Breyers, or Blue Bell?

I called my wife approximately 37 times the other day. I was at the grocery store — sent there, by her, to "pick up a few things" while she finished up homework with the kids and prepped the water to boil for our spaghetti noodles…

RING-RING

"Hello?"
"Hey, babe. Do we get thin spaghetti or angel hair or what?"
"Um. Let's go with angel hair. Ben likes thin noodles."
"OK, cool. Thanks."
"My pleasure."

CLICK
:38 seconds…

RING-RING

"Hello?"
"You said to get 'angel hair', but then you said, 'thin'. Which is it?"
"I said, get angel hair."
"OK. But 'Ben likes thin', you said."
"Right. Angel hair is thin."
"But there's thin spaghetti, too."
"It's called 'thin', but Ben likes angel hair."
"…K"
"Just get the angel hair."
"Got it."
"And don't forget bread."
"OK. See you in a few minutes."
"Bye. Love you."
"Love you, too."

CLICK
:19 seconds…

RING-RING

"Yes?"
"White bread or wheat bread?"
"Italian bread."
"Huh?"
"Get Italian bread."
"Oh."
"We're having spaghetti. We need bread for the spaghetti."
"Oooooh. I thought you meant sandwich bread. Got it."
"OK."
"See you in a few."
"OK."
"OK. Love you."
"Love you ,too."

CLICK
:47 seconds…

RING-RING

"Really?"
"Sorry. Last thing."
"What?"
"You just wrote 'cheese' on the list."
"Parmesan Cheese."
"OK. You didn't put 'Parmesan', so…"
"We're having spaghetti. We need parmesan cheese for the spaghetti."
"Yep. Got it. Anything else?"
"Nope. Just the stuff on the list."
"Cool. And when you wrote salad…"
"Caesar Salad!"
"In the bag?"
"In the what?"
"In the bag?"
"Caesar Salad. Yes… In the bag."

"Perfect. See you in a few minutes. Love you"

"......"

CLICK
:29 seconds…

RING-RING

"For godsakes, Billy."
"Sorry! Just wondering if we need drinks."
"We have drinks."
"Do we have tea? Because tea is on sale."
"I know tea is on sale."
"Do you want for me to get some?"
"Is it on the list?"
"No. But I didn't know if you knew it was on sale."
"I did know that it is on sale."
"But you didn't put it on the list."
"Because we don't need tea."
"We have tea?"
"No."
"But…"
"You know what? Get tea."
"Really?"
"Sure."
"OK. One or two gallons?"

CLICK
:06 seconds…

RING-RING

"Whaaat?!"
"Sorry! You didn't answer me."
"What?!"
"One or two gallons?"
"....."
"Hello?"

"One."

"One?"

"Yep."

"For all of us?"

"We have drinks!"

"OK! Jeez! I'll see you in a few minutes! I lov…"

CLICK
19 minutes

RING-RING

"Hello?"

"Hey. Are you OK?"

"What?"

"Are you OK?"

"I'm fine. Where are you?"

"Because you don't sound OK."

"I'm fine. Where are you?"

At the store."

*"You're **still** at the store?"*

"Yeah, why?"

"It's been almost an hour!"

"Well, you didn't put what kind of ice cream, so I've been looking."

"For ice cream?"

"Yeah."

"Did you find it? Aisle 7."

"Yes. I found it. How did you…"

"Are you on your way home?"

"Not yet."

"Why not!?"

"I.…"

"Hello?!"

"Y….."

"Hello?!

"What kind of…"
"Vanilla! Get vanilla."
"OK. That's all you had to say. I'll be home in a few minutes."
"Bye."
"B…"

CLICK
3 minutes

RING-RING

"…."
"Breyers, or Blue Bell?"

CLICK

She loves me very much. I complete her, I think.

THE BEST
WAY TO LIVE
YOUR BEST
STORY IS TO
UNDERSTAND
YOUR ROLE
IN HELPING
OTHERS LIVE
THEIRS. :)

YOU ARE
THE MOST
AMAZING
KID ON THE
PLANET!
OH, WAIT.
WRONG
LUNCHBOX.
MY BAD.
:-(

Keep 'em guessing.

ONE OUT OF
EVERY FIVE KIDS IN
THE U.S. WILL
COMMIT A CRIME BY
THE TIME THEY TURN
18. I'M PUTTING
ALL MY MONEY ON
YOUR BROTHER.

This is a safe bet. I'm not going to name names, but if you've ever met my family, or have been one of the several thousand people who have witnessed my family trying to navigate Disney with this particular future inmate, you'd know. *Oh, you'd know.*

I WAS KIDDING
LAST NIGHT.
A HYPOTENUSE
IS NOT A
MYTHOLOGICAL
BIRD. HOWEVER,
I WILL GIVE YOU
A DOLLAR IF
YOU PUT THAT
ON YOUR TEST.

Truth be told, I still don't know what a hypotenuse is, but "a birdlike creature with 13 eyes, arms like a man, and horns where it's ears should be" is as accurate an answer as I could come up with.

Some of these notes have layers, y'all.
Like a dad joke parfait with humor and encouragement
in the middle. Others are like this one.

THIS LUNCH WAS MADE WITH U IN MIND. OTHER-WISE IT WOULD BE YOUR LNCH, AND THAT DOESN'T MAKE ANY SENSE.

SOMETIMES,
I SAY CUSS
WORDS WHEN
YOU MAKE ME
ANGRY, AND
I AM SORRY
ABOUT THAT.
OTHER TIMES,
I AM PERFECTLY
FINE WITH IT.
:(

My mother used to say that only ignorant people use profanity. Turns out I can be pretty stupid when my daughter breaks curfew (again) or my son — not the good ones, the other one — still hasn't picked up his wet towel off of the @*%ing floor even though I've asked him nicely 13 times and then he rolls his eyes and mumbles something under his breath.

Go team, go.

Being a parent is hard. Especially for moms. Now, I'm not 100% positive this is true because I have a penis, but as the father of five I can say with great confidence and conviction that Mom'ing has got to be the most difficult thing in the world.

I'm not a biologist or psychologist or anyone worth quoting, really, but you can trust me. I had a Mom, I know a lot of Moms, and I snore next to one of them—the best one, in my opinion—every night. That last fact alone is proof enough that the female sex endures the most harrowing existence there is, and that the Mom, *the Mom*, is the strongest and bravest and smartest and most formidable of the species without even a shadow of a doubt.

Being a dad is like being an assistant coach on a professional basketball team. I work kind of hard, I guess. I've got a clipboard with all the rules on it. I yell a lot and wave my arms, and look pretty busy on the sidelines with my shiny shoes and ten dollar haircut. I shake my head disapprovingly sometimes, but mostly I just give high-fives and slap people on the butt as they walk past, not listening to a single word I say.

Taking the basketball analogy excruciatingly too far, I imagine that being a mom is like being the head coach, lead cheerleader, star player, mascot, team owner, chief executive officer of basketball and gameday operations, *and* the ball... all at once.

I guess what I am trying to say is that the mom my children came out of is pretty special. And I'm not just writing that here because she's my wife and I'm a little bit scared of her; I write it because it's true.

She is gorgeous and wonderful and perfect in almost every way. She's someone that catches your breath and your heart, and you oftentimes get overcome by the simple fact that you share the same planet as this beautiful creature. She's the everything, but willing to become the nothing so that everyone around her can shine a little brighter. She's the real deal and the reason I smile most of the time, and I just thought you should know.

Actually, I don't smile most of the time—because I am a parent and being a parent is hard—but when I do smile, it's usually because of my favorite Mom.

Go team, go.

Hungry?

I
LOVE
KISSING
YOUR
MOM.
ANYWAY,
ENJOY
YOUR
LUNCH.

I BELIEVE THE BEST CHEESE IS THE "PUFF," DON'T YOU?

According to historians, philosophers and other smart people who research food and stuff, cheese evidently became a sophisticated enterprise at the start of the ancient Rome era when valued foreign cheeses were transported to Italy to satisfy the tastes of the social elite. I bet the puff, though, was invented by a guy named "Darrell" with two 'l's' in the kitchenette of his doublewide trailer that also served as his fireworks stand in the summertime.

God bless you, Darrell.

I have five kids. They've each received this note several times. A couple of them probably even believe it's true.

YOU'RE
MY
FAVORITE.
PLEASE

DON'T
TELL
THE

OTHERS.

I HOPE YOU
APPRECIATE
HOW AWESOME
YOU ARE,
BECAUSE I'VE
HAD A LOT
TO DO WITH
THAT. :)

"Give credit where credit is due." That's what I always say. I also like to say stuff like "Honesty is the best policy," so with those things in mind I should probably replace "I've" on this napkin with "your mom," but we get on to the kids when they say "your mom," so I guess we're gonna have to keep this as-is.

I don't like cats. They're mean. They're selfish. They poop in a box of gravel that we keep in the garage. They're disgusting creatures. Not at all like dogs. Dogs snuggle. They jump up on. They give you kisses and lick your face… you know, after they lick them-*selves* and hump your leg and what-not.

Anyway, I love dogs so much I don't even think twice about carrying a bag of their poop while they pull me up and down the street on a leash in front of my neighbors. Dogs rule.

THE SAME CAT
YOU LET SLEEP
WITH YOU AND
LICK YOUR FACE
EATS CHIPMUNKS
AND DRINKS
TOILET WATER.
ANYWAY, ENJOY
THE REST OF
YOUR DAY.
:-(

WONDER
ALWAYS,
AND
YOU
WILL
STAY
WONDER-
FUL.

This probably isn't true. In fact, I'm kind of tired of all the questions. My daughter once asked, "Hey, dad. Why do dogs don't have no lips?" Now, that is either the worst formed question I have ever heard, or the best. I can't be sure. If dogs *don't* have *no* lips, that means they actually *do* have lips. But *do* they *don't* have no lips?

Or *don't* they? See what I mean? Kids are dumb.

A strange, dull headache.

Screams came from the hallway this morning at 6:39 AM: *"Oh, my gosh! Dude! What the… Oh, gross. What's that smell!"*

I heard one kid gagging at another kid.

"What!?"

The other kid shot back — the way a guilty man might feign being offended at being asked where he was the night of November such and such in 1983.

"Dude, it's your backpack. What the crap is that?"

The first kid was appalled and literally gagging now.

Pulling away and trying not to make eye contact with anyone, Stinky looked toward the ground and simply shrugged his shoulders.

I stepped into the hallway and it hit me.

"Sweet Lord. What's in there?" My throat tightened.

"I don't know," he whispered, still looking down.

"Well, have… you… checked?!" My voice was getting higher and louder with every syllable.

Knowing that he was defeated, he dropped the backpack at my feet and slinked away. The smell was sour and musty, but also sweet; like a flooded basement full of old lip gloss.

I unzipped the bag.

Over the winter break — a day short of three entire weeks — a lot of things occurred: *Countless Christmas gatherings, parties, concerts, shopping trips, hiking trips, card games, movies, a weekend jaunt to Atlanta to see my brother and his family, and — good grief — we even went on a cruise. All seven of us. From Mobile, Alabama to Cozumel, Mexico and back home again. We visited a whole 'nother country a couple of weeks ago! It was a pretty remarkable break. My goodness, we even rang in a brand new year!*

A remarkable break, indeed.

And while all of that was happening: the gatherings and parties, and family adventures and what-not; this backpack... A blue one, with gray piping and big, white, stitched, block letters that read: "QUINN"... sat in the corner of a closet... festering.

Have you ever almost fallen down because of a smell? I hadn't either until this morning. My knees buckled and I dropped the bag, grasping for the wall to hold me.

I guess he just wasn't hungry the day I packed the Turkey and Cheese sandwich, raspberries, yogurt cup, Doritos, fruit snacks, and chocolate milk, because the lunch sack remained — smashed and leaking — exactly where he had shoved it back in mid-December. Last month. Last year.

He's on the bus now, unbruised (by God's grace) and unfazed. His backpack is in the washer. I have a strange, dull headache. And I'm going back to bed...

I've seen them eat boogers. Surely they can muscle through an "overdue" cheese stick every now and then.

DON'T
WORRY
ABOUT
THE
EXPIRATION
DATE.
I'M
PRETTY
SURE
THAT'S A
MISPRINT.

IF I HAD A NICKEL FOR EVERY TIME I SAID I WAS GONNA START EATING BETTER, I COULD BUY, LIKE, 37 CHEESEBURGERS.

I've never been good at word problems.

Some animals, like squirrels, mice, teenage boys, and beavers gather extra supplies in the fall and store them to use later... My 16-year-old has evidently been readying for an impending winter apocalypse over the past 7-12 years.

PLEASE CLEAN
YOUR ROOM.
I CAN'T FIND
ANY OF OUR
BOWLS, FORKS,
CUPS, SPOONS,
TUPPERWARE,
TOWELS, SOCKS,
OR THE
PEANUT BUTTER.

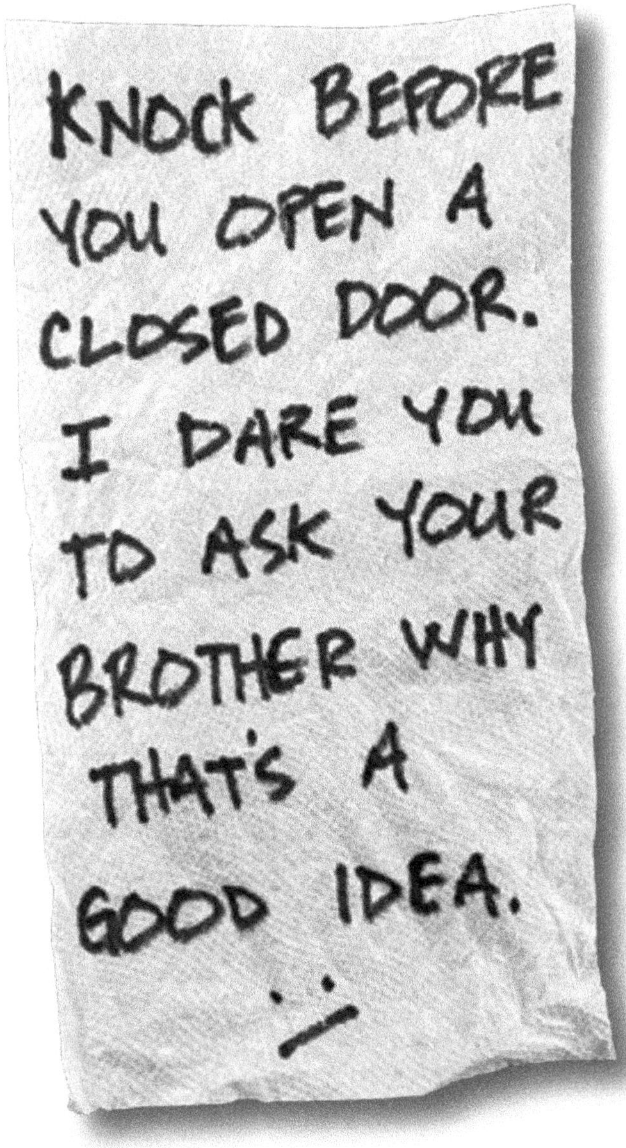
KNOCK BEFORE
YOU OPEN A
CLOSED DOOR.
I DARE YOU
TO ASK YOUR
BROTHER WHY
THAT'S A
GOOD IDEA.
:-/

I mean, if you really think about it, loving somebody even *four* ways is kind of a lot. Or three, for that matter.

OH, HOW I
LOVE YOU!
LET ME COUNT
THE WAYS...
SEVEN! NO,
WAIT, SIX!
I LOVE YOU
APPROXIMATELY
SIX WAYS.
OK, FIVE.

YOU DON'T
HAVE TO
DO WORLD-
CHANGING
THINGS
TO CHANGE
THE WORLD.

Think about the most influential person in your life — the person who has had the biggest impact on you. Chances are, that person hasn't walked on the moon or cured cancer or accumulated hundreds of millions of dollars, or even a boatload of followers on social media. More than likely that person is just a normal guy or girl. Someone who made good on the opportunity to love you well, tell you the truth, and invest time and attention (intentionally) in things that matter to you. *For* you. You don't have to do world-changing things to change the world. Sometimes, you've just gotta show up.

Why is it so easy to forget… so hard to remember… that the people who love us most are the same people who know all the things that we think might make us unlovable?

YOU
ARE
SEEN.
YOU
ARE
KNOWN.
YOU
ARE
LOVED
ANYWAY.

ATTITUDE
IS
EVERYTHING.
TODAY IS
NOT YET
ANYTHING.
FILL IT
WITH
LAUGHTER.

My father gave me the precious gift of perspective when he wrote me those words before he died. This simple, but beautiful lesson was never intended to change my life. He just wanted to change my day. And he did. Over and over and over again.

"If the weather calls for rain, decide now that you will enjoy getting wet…"

Perspective changes everything, y'all.

Attitude is everything.
Today is not yet anything.
Fill it with laughter.

July 11, 1988. 16 days before my 16th birthday. That was the day my father went to heaven. He had ALS. Lou Gehrig's Disease.

Good grief, that sounds like a long time ago when you say it out loud, but that day — *that day* — still seems like it was this week.

I remember what I was wearing when I found him. I remember

what I did as soon as I knew: *I ran out the back door of the house and into the back yard, screaming obscenities, trying to make myself cry.*

I don't really recall a lot after that; the days that followed, or even the funeral. Those memories play back like scenes from television reruns. Bits and pieces seem clear, but most of the dialogue is paraphrased, muffled, or blurred.

I do remember his mustache — he had a great Tom Selleck mustache that would disappear into his coffee cup, and it stung my face when he kissed me goodnight or gave me a "zerbert" before school.

I remember his laugh.
And I remember his eyes.
He had happy eyes.

As I grow older, the more and more thankful I am for my Dad

and the influence he had on my childhood. But I think I am *most* thankful for the impact he has had on me since he's been gone.

Let me explain:

After people die we tend to remember the best of them. And as time passes, memories play back like a "Best of…" highlight reel. You know, like a "one shining Moment montage at the end of the NCAA basketball tournament?

Not many people sit around and ponder the douchey things their dead relatives did. And even then, there's a kindness and fondness to the memory.

My memories of my father are all good ones. I'm sure he yelled sometimes, but I don't remember. And I bet he had a good reason if he did. Probably my sister.

I'm sure he had annoying habits and flaws that bothered me and others. I'm sure he smelled bad from time to time. But I can't recall.

I just remember him being there. At practices, games, performances, church and the dinner table. I remember his smile. I remember playing football in the front yard, wrestling, skipping rocks and skipping *church* to watch John McEnroe defeat Bjorn Borg in the 1981 Wimbledon championship. I was nine. And *that* was awesome.

He sounded kind of like a seal being eaten by a larger seal when he laughed. *Honk! Honk! Honk!* He'd listen so intently as I recounted silly stories or made-up jokes and then he'd belly

laugh as if I were the funniest 14-year-old on the planet.
I remember singing at the top of our lungs in his Jeep:
You picked a fine time to leeeeave me Luciiiillle...

I don't remember a single time when he was disappointed or angry. I don't remember him telling me to get my shoes out of the middle of the floor or to go make my bed. Of course he did all of those things, but that's not who he was. He was the guy who taught me how to juggle by tossing around pieces of my grandmother's fine china. The man who threw me flailing through the air at the swimming pool, and then again and again, because, "I think I can get you farther out there this time." He was the one who let me ride on his shoulders while climbing Stone Mountain. The guy who sweated through telling about how men and women are different and how babies are made when those "differences" bump into each other.

I remember that my dad ran a lot. He was a marathon runner, actually. But I don't have a clear memory of him *actually* running.

Not a single one.

He loved Jesus, and he loved to tell people about how God had changed his life. After he got sick, he was even more excited and vocal about God's love and grace. I remember getting frustrated about that. I was a healthy, confused, and pissed off teenager, and he was about to die with those happy eyes.

I didn't get it back then. I do now.

My story — like all stories — is full of major and minor characters that have impacted me in one way or another. Like the lady I saw in the checkout line at Wal-Mart this weekend. She was a *minor* character. True, I will not soon forget the chain she had connected to rings in her ear and her nose, but she simply made an impression.

My father, on the other hand, was a *major* character. Someone around whom the plot of my story has been cast. He helped shape me, mold me, guide me, and direct me to where my story will ultimately lead.

I'm getting to a point, I promise.

We all have a unique opportunity to help shape the people around us. Every day we're here. The things we do and the memories we create – no matter how faded or heightened they become over time – can make a real, meaningful, and forever-difference in the stories of folks we love. And here's the really great part: *We don't have to do great, big things to make a difference.*

Quick story:

I got cut from my school's basketball team in eighth grade, and I was devastated. Truth be told, I *should* have been cut because I wasn't very good. But my dad knew I was upset, and he ached with me. Later on that day, he proceeded to give me one of the the single, greatest gifts he had ever given me. That night, after I had gone to bed, he wrote me a note. It was scribbled, and hard to make out because he had to write it with his left hand. He was born right-handed, but the disease had rendered his right arm useless. So, he sat down at the kitchen table that night and wrote this with his left:

Hey buddy.

Today is going to be a great day. It's your day.
No one and nothing can make your day anything other than
what you want it to be. If the weather calls for rain, decide
now that you will enjoy being wet. If the test score is low, work
hard to make sure the next one is higher. If treated unfairly
for something, smile and be thankful for the many things
you've not been caught for.

Attitude is everything.
Today is not yet anything.
Fill it with laughter.
—Dad

I kept that note for a long time. Somewhere along the way, I
lost the original, but the *idea* of that note — and the words he
wrote — have stuck with me. Hardly a week goes by that I don't
think about him and what he must've been going through when
he took the time to encourage me and reveal some truth about
what really matters.

It was such a simple act, but the mark it made on me is indelible.

Now, I may not remember all the details of my relationship
with the man I called "Dad," but I hope that the life he helped
shape can become a meaningful character in the story of others.

I write silly stuff on napkins. What's *your* story?

That's all, folks.